GREATEST OF ALL TIME PLAYERS

G.O.A.T. FOOTBALL DEFENSIVE LINEMEN

Josh Anderson

Lerner Publications ◆ Minneapolis

SPORTS THRILLS *MEET* **RESEARCH SKILLS**

Lerner **SPORTS**

Free Database Trial: **lernersports.com**

Lerner Publications Company
An imprint of Lerner Publishing Group, Inc.
241 First Avenue North
Minneapolis, MN 55401 USA

For reading levels and more information, look up this title at www.lernerbooks.com.

Main body text set in Aptifer Sans LT Pro.
Typeface provided by Linotype AG.

Library of Congress Cataloging-in-Publication Data

Names: Anderson, Josh, author.
Title: G.O.A.T. football defensive linemen / Josh Anderson.
Other titles: Greatest of all time defensive linemen
Description: Minneapolis, MN : Lerner Publications , [2024]. | Series: Lerner sports. Greatest of all time players | Includes bibliographical references and index. | Audience: Ages 7–11 | Audience: Grades 2–3 | Summary: "In the NFL, defensive linemen are often the biggest, meanest players on the team. Find out how the best linemen were so good at sacking quarterbacks, batting down passes, and manhandling running backs"— Provided by publisher.
Identifiers: LCCN 2023017452 (print) | LCCN 2023017453 (ebook) | ISBN 9798765610220 (library binding) | ISBN 9798765623589 (paperback) | ISBN 9798765614785 (epub)
Subjects: LCSH: Football players—United States—Biography—Juvenile literature. | Football—Defense—Juvenile literature. | BISAC: JUVENILE NONFICTION / Biography & Autobiography / Sports & Recreation
Classification: LCC GV939.A1 A527 2024 (print) | LCC GV939.A1 (ebook) | DDC 796.332092/2 [B]—dc23/eng/20230515

LC record available at https://lccn.loc.gov/2023017452
LC ebook record available at https://lccn.loc.gov/2023017453

Manufactured in the United States of America
1 – CG – 12/15/23

TABLE OF CONTENTS

BATTLE AT THE LINE OF SCRIMMAGE

The Green Bay Packers were close to winning the 1997 Super Bowl. The New England Patriots had the ball with under two minutes to play. They were hoping to cut the Packers' 14-point lead. But one big defensive play by Green Bay would put the game nearly out of reach.

FACTS AT A GLANCE

» **AARON DONALD** HELPED THE LOS ANGELES RAMS WIN THE 2022 SUPER BOWL BY SACKING CINCINNATI BENGALS QUARTERBACK JOE BURROW ON ONE OF THE GAME'S LAST PLAYS.

» **REGGIE WHITE** HOLDS THE NATIONAL FOOTBALL LEAGUE (NFL) RECORD WITH NINE STRAIGHT SEASONS WITH AT LEAST 11 SACKS.

» THE NFL BEGAN RECORDING **SACKS** AS AN OFFICIAL STAT IN 1982. ALL SACKS THAT TOOK PLACE BEFORE THEN ARE UNOFFICIAL.

» **BRUCE SMITH'S** 200 CAREER SACKS ARE THE MOST IN NFL HISTORY.

Packers defensive lineman Reggie White set up for the play on the left side of the line. He already had two sacks in the game. White had achieved so much in his long career. But he had never won a Super Bowl.

Patriots quarterback Drew Bledsoe took the ball and looked for an open teammate. White rushed toward Bledsoe. White grabbed the quarterback's legs and threw him to the ground for a sack. The Super Bowl ended a few plays later. Green Bay won the game 35–21. White's three-sack performance in the Super Bowl was one of the greatest of his amazing career.

Defensive linemen try to push past the offensive line on passing plays. They try to sack the quarterback or force them into making a mistake. Sacks didn't count as an official NFL stat until 1982. All sacks that took place before then are unofficial.

On running plays, defensive linemen try to stop the runner before he can make a big gain. Another stat used to measure defensive players is forced fumbles. A forced fumble is when a hit from a defender causes an offensive player to drop the football. A fumble can allow the defending team to take control of the ball.

During games, the offensive line and the defensive line battle at the line of scrimmage. Many players and coaches think this battle is the key to success on the football field. The

The Kansas City Chiefs defensive line (*left*) faces off against the Bengals offensive line (*right*) during a 2003 playoff game.

Aaron Donald (*center left*) blocks a pass from Tampa Bay Buccaneers quarterback Tom Brady (*center*) in a 2022 game.

team that controls the line of scrimmage often wins the game.

Defensive tackles play near the middle of the defensive line. They are often the largest players on the defense. Defensive ends play on the ends of the line. They often try to run around the offensive line, so they are usually smaller and faster than defensive tackles.

Defensive linemen are very important to a team's success. But they don't get as much attention as other positions, such as quarterback. Only one defensive lineman has ever won the NFL Most Valuable Player (MVP) award. Alan Page of the Minnesota Vikings won it in 1971. Keep reading to learn more about football's G.O.A.T., the greatest of all time.

MICHAEL STRAHAN

Michael Strahan played all 15 of his NFL seasons for the New York Giants. From 1993 to 2007, he was one of the best defensive ends in the NFL. In 2001, he set a season record when he totaled 22.5 sacks. Strahan was the NFL's sack leader again in 2003. He led the league three times in tackles behind the line of scrimmage, resulting in lost yards. Strahan was a key part of New York's victory over the Patriots in the 2008 Super Bowl. He had a sack and three tackles in the game.

After his playing career ended, Strahan entered the Pro Football Hall of Fame. He has also found great success on TV. Strahan has worked as a host on *Good Morning America, Live! With Kelly and Michael, FOX NFL Sunday,* and *The $100,000 Pyramid.*

MICHAEL STRAHAN STATS

	Games Played	216
	Sacks	141.5
	Forced Fumbles	24
	Pro Bowls	7

J. J. WATT

J. J. Watt played in 12 NFL seasons for the Houston Texans and Arizona Cardinals. He was strong and fast enough to play both defensive end and defensive tackle. Sometimes he even played offense. In 2014, he caught three touchdown passes.

From 2012 to 2015, Watt was among the top players in the NFL. He won the league's Defensive Player of the Year award three times. Watt also led the league in sacks in 2012 and 2015. He led the league in tackles behind the line of scrimmage three times.

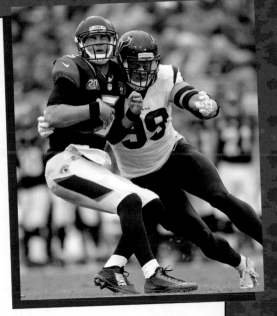

In 2017, a hurricane caused a great amount of damage to Houston, Texas, and nearby areas. Watt helped to raise more than $37 million for hurricane relief. He only played in five games that year, but Watt won the *Sports Illustrated* Sportsperson of the Year award for his efforts to help families affected by the hurricane.

J. J. WATT STATS

🏈	Games Played	151
🏈	Sacks	114.5
🏈	Forced Fumbles	27
🏈	Pro Bowls	5

Julius Peppers was a star athlete before he ever set foot on an NFL field. He played both football and basketball for the University of North Carolina Tar Heels. Peppers even helped lead the Tar Heels to college basketball's Final Four in 2000.

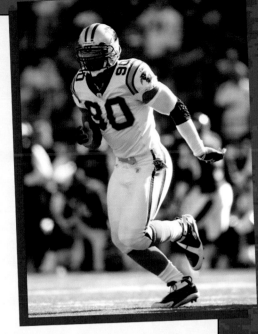

Peppers played 10 of his 17 NFL seasons for the Carolina Panthers. He won the NFL's Defensive Rookie of the Year award in 2002 after totaling 12 sacks and five forced fumbles. Peppers used his size, strength, and speed to make life hard for opposing teams.

His 159.5 sacks rank fifth all-time. He also ranks second in NFL history with 52 forced fumbles. And he ranks third all-time with 175 tackles behind the line of scrimmage. Peppers never won a Super Bowl, but he helped lead Carolina to the big game in 2004. The Panthers lost 32–29 to the Patriots.

JULIUS PEPPERS STATS

Games Played	266
Sacks	159.5
Forced Fumbles	52
Pro Bowls	9

MERLIN OLSEN

Merlin Olsen played all 15 of his NFL seasons for the
Los Angeles Rams. He missed two games during his first
season in 1962. Olsen then played in every Rams game for
the next 14 years.

Olsen was a strong and skilled player. But fans also
remember him for being smart on the field. He was one of
the leaders of the Rams defense. Defensive linemen Olsen,

Deacon Jones, Rosey Grier, and Lamar Lundy were known as the Fearsome Foursome.

Two of Olsen's brothers also played in the NFL. Merlin Olsen and his brother Phil Olsen were teammates in Los Angeles from 1971 to 1974. Their brother Orrin Olsen played one season for the Kansas City Chiefs. After his football career, Merlin Olsen played a farmer on the popular TV show *Little House on the Prairie*.

Olsen joined the Pro Football Hall of Fame in 1982. In 2019, he became a member of the NFL's 100th Anniversary All-Time Team. The team honored the best players in league history.

MERLIN OLSEN STATS

Games Played	208
Sacks	91
Forced Fumbles	9
Pro Bowls	14

AARON DONALD

Aaron Donald has played his entire NFL career for the Rams. He spent his first two seasons with the team in St. Louis, Missouri. When the Rams moved back to Los Angeles, California, in 2016, Donald moved with them. He has won the NFL's Defensive Player of the Year award three times. In 2018, he led the league with 20.5 sacks. He has led the league in tackles behind the line of scrimmage twice. And Donald was a Pro Bowl player after each of his first nine seasons in the NFL.

After losing the 2019 Super Bowl to the Patriots, the Rams made it back to the big game in 2022. Donald tackled Cincinnati Bengals quarterback Joe Burrow on one of the game's final plays. The tackle helped seal the victory for Los Angeles. It was the first Super Bowl win for the Rams in more than 20 years.

AARON DONALD STATS

🏈	Games Played	138
🏈	Sacks	103
🏈	Forced Fumbles	24
🏈	Pro Bowls	9

Stats are accurate through the 2022 NFL season.

JOE GREENE

Joe Greene played college football for the University of North Texas in the 1960s. The athletic teams at the school are called the Mean Green. Greene's teammates started calling him "Mean" Joe Greene. He was a strong player and made life difficult for opposing teams. The nickname followed Greene to the NFL.

Greene played all 13 of his NFL seasons for the Pittsburgh Steelers. His strength and skill made him one of the league's toughest defenders. He was the leader of the Steel Curtain defense that led Pittsburgh to four Super Bowl victories from 1975 to 1980. Greene won the league's Defensive Player of the Year award twice.

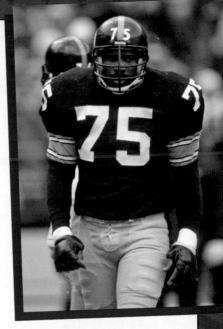

The Steelers retired Greene's number 75 jersey in 2014. In Greene's honor, no Steelers player will ever wear that number again. Greene became part of the Pro Football Hall of Fame in 1987. In 2019, the NFL picked Greene as a member of its 100th Anniversary All-Time Team.

JOE GREENE STATS

Games Played	181
Sacks	77.5
Defensive Player of the Year Awards	2
Pro Bowls	10

ALAN PAGE

Alan Page used his speed to attack opposing ballcarriers. In 1971, he became the first defensive player to win the NFL's MVP award. Page and Lawrence Taylor are the only defenders to ever win it.

As part of the Purple People Eaters defensive line, Page helped the Minnesota Vikings reach four Super Bowls in the

1970s. The Purple People Eaters nickname came from the team's uniform color and the defensive line's strength and success. Few quarterbacks could get past them.

Page won the league's Defensive Player of the Year award twice. After retiring in 1981, Page joined the Pro Football Hall of Fame and became a Minnesota Supreme Court justice. As a justice, Page helped decide the state's most important legal cases.

ALAN PAGE STATS

 Games Played | 218

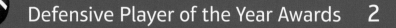 Sacks | 148.5

Defensive Player of the Year Awards | 2

 Pro Bowls | 9

DEACON JONES

When Deacon Jones entered the 1961 NFL Draft, teams didn't see him as a top player. They chose 185 other players before the Los Angeles Rams chose him in the 14th round. Most players chosen that late have short careers. But Jones played in 14 NFL seasons, including 11 with the Rams.

Sacks were not an official stat when Jones played, but he led the NFL in unofficial sacks five times. He even coined the word *sack*. He based the idea on wrapping the quarterback in his arms, like putting him in a sack.

Jones was part of the Fearsome Foursome defensive line. The four Rams players earned this nickname by crashing through offensive lines. Jones finished his career with 173.5 sacks, third-most all-time. Jones became part of the Pro Football Hall of Fame in 1980. In 2019, the NFL picked Jones for its 100th Anniversary All-Time Team.

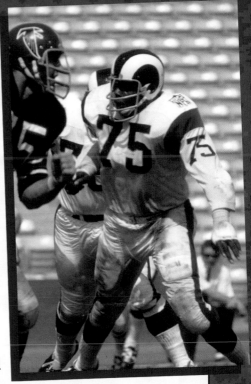

DEACON JONES STATS

Games Played	191
Sacks	173.5
Forced Fumbles	22
Pro Bowls	8

BRUCE SMITH

Bruce Smith was drafted first overall in the 1985 NFL Draft by the Buffalo Bills. He played 15 of his 19 NFL seasons with Buffalo. Smith helped lead the team to four Super Bowl appearances in a row from 1991 to 1994.

Smith was so strong that star quarterback Warren Moon compared his strength to a bulldozer. Smith never led the NFL in sacks, but he had at least 10 sacks in 13 different seasons. His 200 career sacks are the most in NFL history. Smith led the league twice in forced fumbles. He was the NFL's Defensive Player of the Year in 1990 and 1996.

After his career, Smith became part of the Pro Football Hall of Fame. The NFL also picked him for its 100th Anniversary All-Time Team.

BRUCE SMITH STATS

🏈	Games Played	279
🏈	Sacks	200
🏈	Forced Fumbles	43
🏈	Pro Bowls	11

REGGIE WHITE

Reggie White used speed and strength to beat opposing offenses for 15 NFL seasons. He was an unstoppable force. Offensive lines hoped to simply slow him down.

White used a wide range of skills on the field. One was the swim move. White swung his arms like a swimmer to push past offensive linemen.

White holds the NFL record with nine straight seasons of at least 11 sacks. He led the league in sacks twice and finished his career with 198, the second-most of all time. White may have been even better against running plays. His speed allowed him to quickly change direction and bring down running backs.

Near the end of his career, White had three sacks in the 1997 Super Bowl. He led the Green Bay Packers to victory. In 2019, White was part of the NFL's 100th Anniversary All-Time Team.

REGGIE WHITE STATS

 Games Played   232

EVEN MORE G.O.A.T.

There have been so many amazing defensive linemen in football history. Choosing only 10 is a challenge. Here are 10 others who could have made the G.O.A.T. list.

....

No. 11   GINO MARCHETTI

No. 12   BOB LILLY

No. 13   RANDY WHITE

No. 14   LEE ROY SELMON

No. 15   DOUG ATKINS

No. 16   BILL HEWITT

No. 17   JOHN RANDLE

No. 18   WARREN SAPP

No. 19   JACK YOUNGBLOOD

No. 20   KEVIN GREENE

YOUR
G.O.A.T.

It's your turn to make a G.O.A.T. list of defensive linemen. If some of your favorite players aren't defensive linemen, make a list for another position too! You can also make G.O.A.T. lists for movies, books, and other things you like.

Start by doing research. You can check out the Learn More section on page 31. The books and websites listed there will help you learn more about football players of the past and present. You can also search online for even more information about great players.

Once you have your list, ask friends and family to create their lists. Compare them and see how they differ. Do your friends have different opinions about the greatest players? Talk it over and decide whose G.O.A.T. list is your favorite.

GLOSSARY

ballcarrier: a football player who carries the ball on offense

defensive line: the players on the defensive side of the line of scrimmage who rush the quarterback and try to stop running plays

fumble: when a football player loses hold of the ball while handling or running with it

justice: a judge

line of scrimmage: an imaginary line that marks the position of the ball at the start of each play

NFL Draft: a yearly event when NFL teams take turns choosing new players

offensive line: the five players on the offensive side of the line of scrimmage who block defenders

Pro Bowl: the NFL's all-star game

rookie: a first-year player

sack: when the quarterback is tackled for a loss of yards

LEARN MORE

Editors of *Sports Illustrated* Kids. *Big Book of WHO Football*. New York: Sports Illustrated, 2022.

Hill, Christina. *Aaron Donald*. Minneapolis: Lerner Publications, 2022.

NFL 100th Anniversary Team: Official All-Time Roster
www.nfl.com/100/all-time-team/roster

Pro Football Hall of Fame
https://www.profootballhof.com

Sarantou, Katlin. *J. J. Watt*. Ann Arbor, MI: Cherry Lake Publishing, 2020.

Sports Illustrated Kids: Football
https://www.sikids.com/football

INDEX

PHOTO ACKNOWLEDGMENTS

Image credits: Focus On Sport/Contributor/Getty Images, p.4; JEFF HAYNES/Staff/Getty Images, p.5; Kevin C. Cox/Staff/Getty Images, p.6; Mike Ehrmann/Staff/Getty Images, p.7; Nick Laham/Staff/Getty Images, p.8; Rob Tringali/Sportschrome/Contributor/Getty Images, p.9; Scott Halleran/Staff/Getty Images, p.10; Rob Foldy/Stringer/Getty Images, p.11; Kevin C. Cox/Staff/Getty Images, p.12; Rob Tringali/Sportschrome/Contributor/Getty Images, p.13; Focus On Sport/Contributor/Getty Images, p.14; Focus On Sport/Contributor/Getty Images, p.15; Sean M. Haffey/Staff/Getty Images, p.16; Focus On Sport/Contributor/Getty Images, p.17; Focus On Sport/Contributor/Getty Images, p.18; George Gojkovich/Contributor/Getty Images, p.19; Focus On Sport/Contributor/Getty Images, p.20; Focus On Sport/Contributor/Getty Images, p.21; Focus On Sport/Contributor/Getty Images, p.22; Focus On Sport/Contributor/Getty Images, 23; Focus On Sport/Contributor/Getty Images, p.24; Focus On Sport/Contributor/Getty Images, p.25; Stephen Dunn/Staff/Getty Images, p.26; Focus On Sport/Contributor/Getty Images, p.27

Cover: Focus On Sport/Contributor/Getty Images; Sporting News Archive/Contributor/Getty Images; Kevin Sabitus/Contributor/Getty Images1